BATTLE LINES

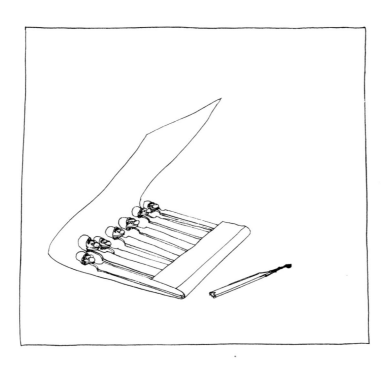

BATTLE LINES

HANS-GEORG RAUCH

CHARLES SCRIBNER'S SONS NEW YORK

Copyright © 1977 Rowohlt Verlag GmbH
This work was published in Germany under the title SCHLACHTLINIEN

Library of Congress Cataloging in Publication Data
Rauch, Hans-Georg, 1939-
    Battle lines.
    Translation of Schlachtlinien.
    1. War—Caricatures and cartoons. 2. German wit and
humor, Pictorial. I. Title.
NC1509.R34A56513   741.5'943   77-8009
ISBN 0-684-15139-1

1 3 5 7 9 11 13 15 17 19 MD/C 20 18 16 14 12 10 8 6 4 2

PRINTED IN THE UNITED STATES OF AMERICA

dedicated to

G.I. JOHN LOCKE

BATTLE
LINES

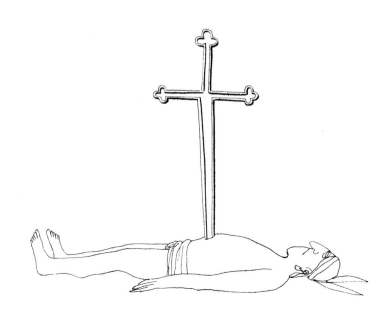

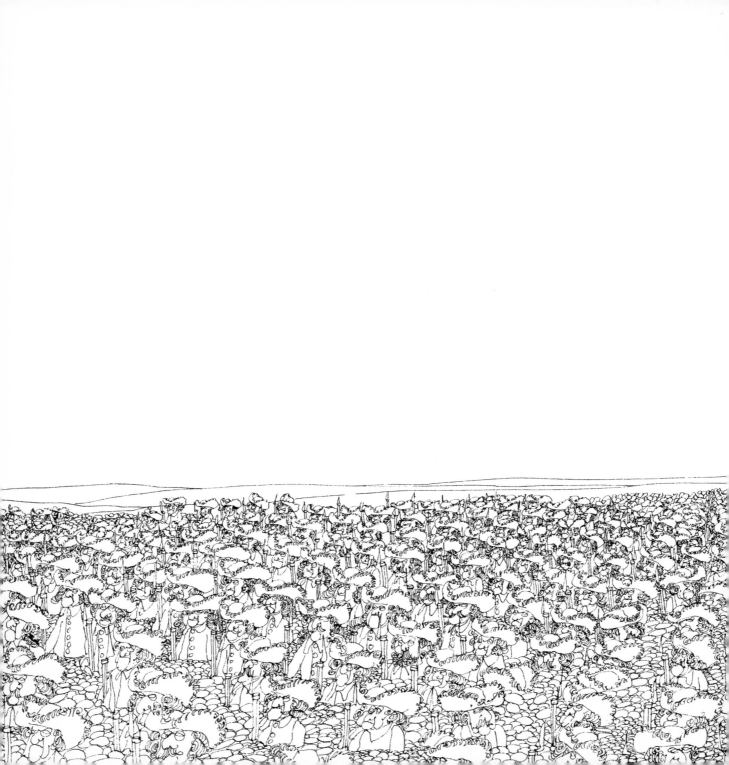

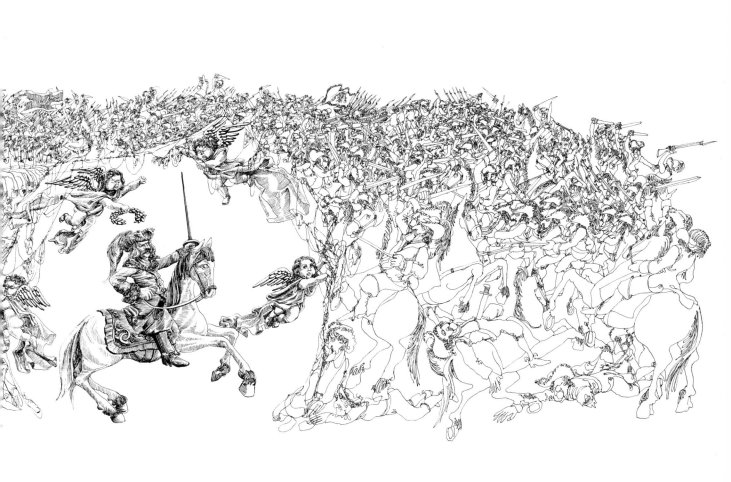

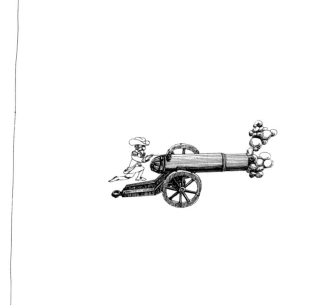

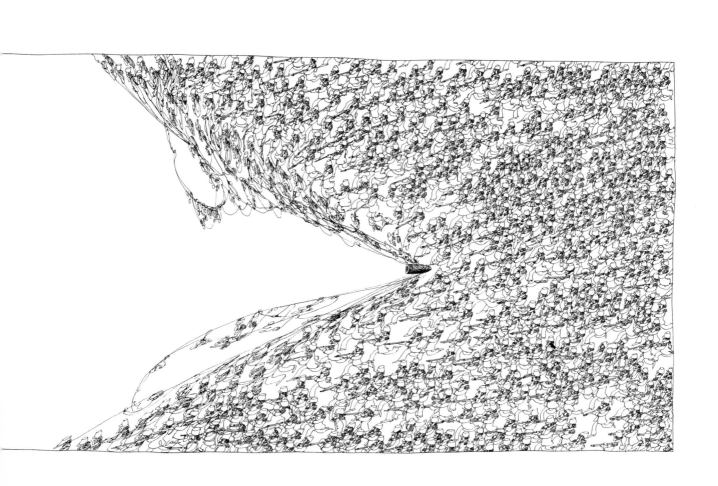

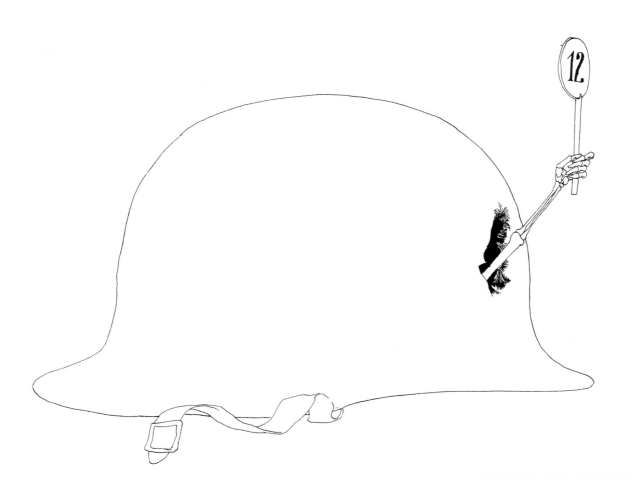

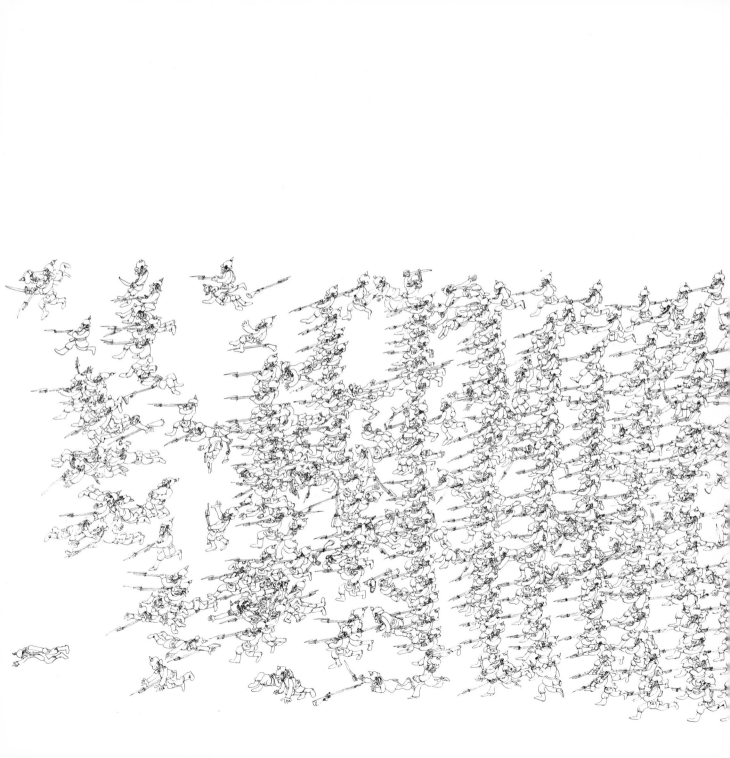

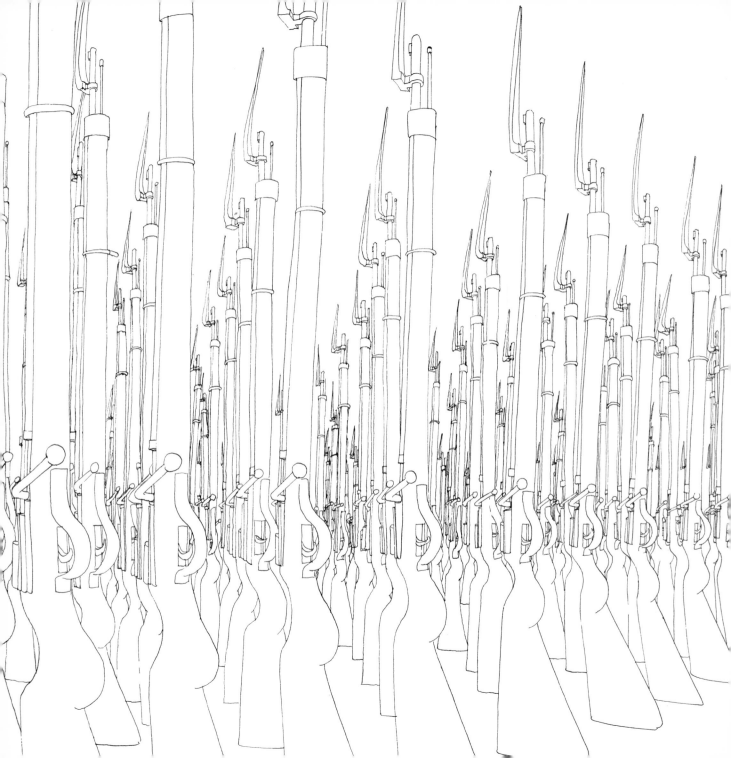

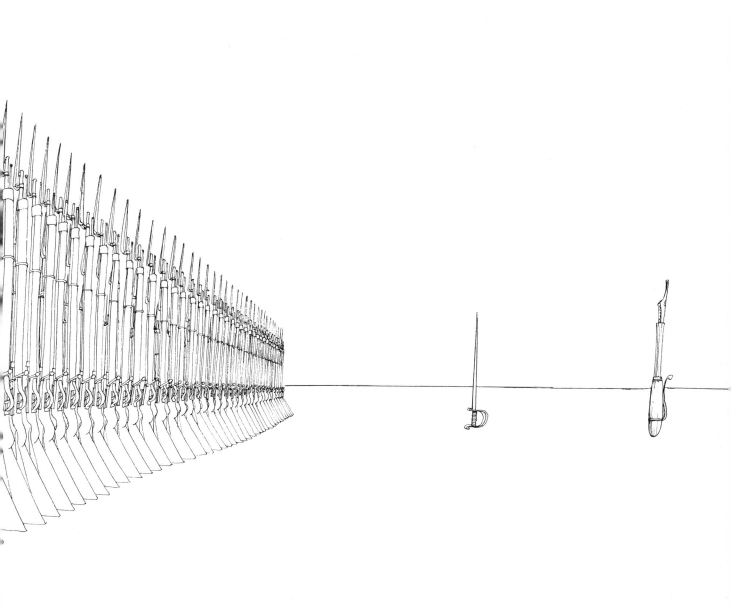

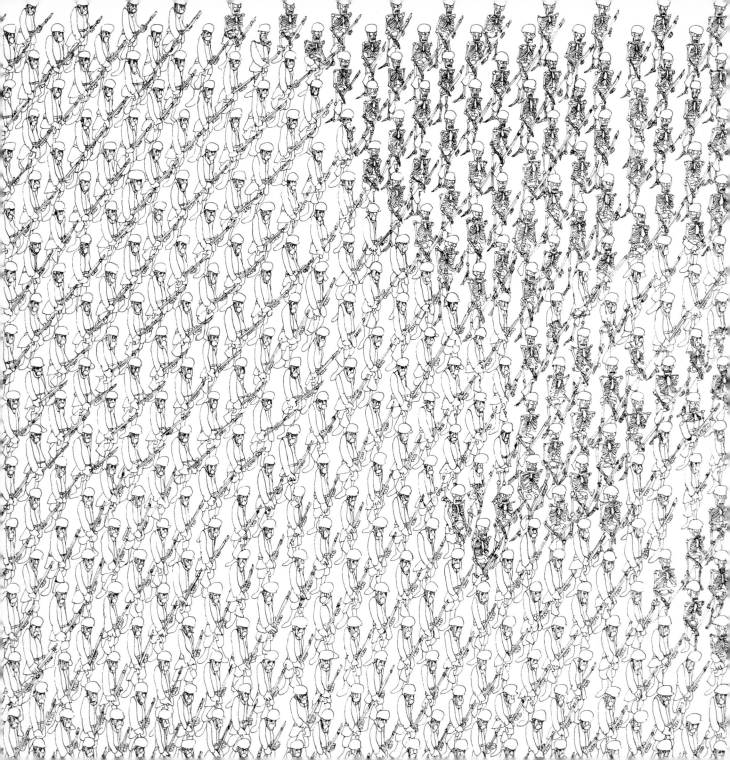

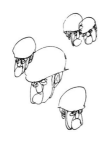

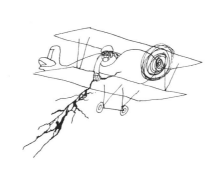

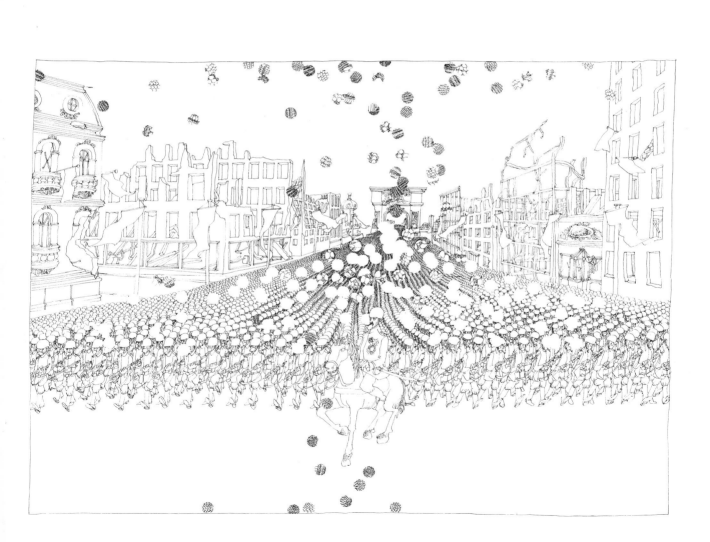

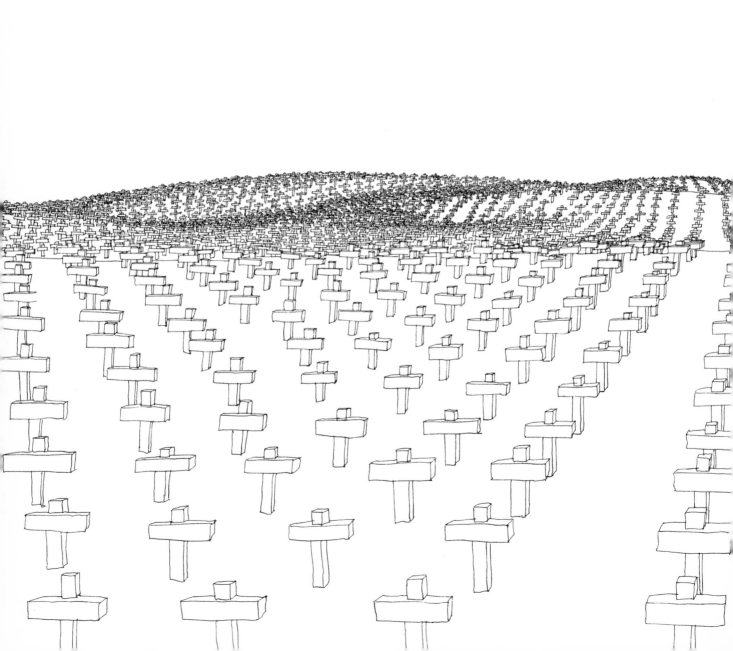

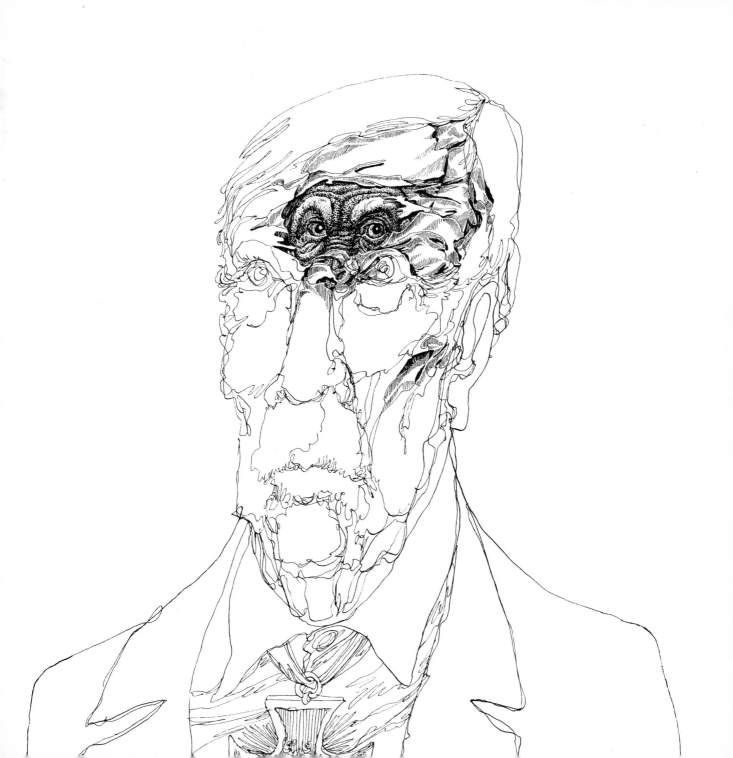

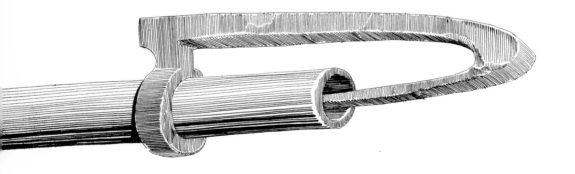

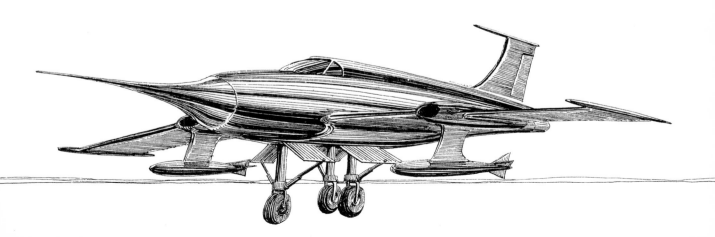

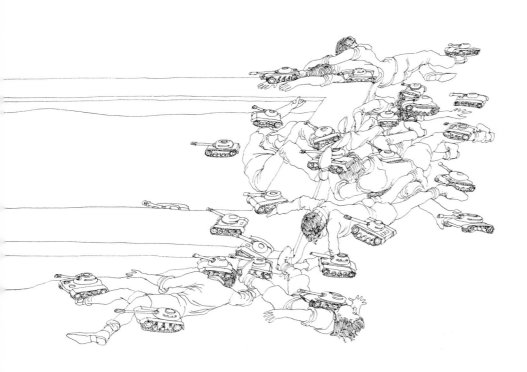

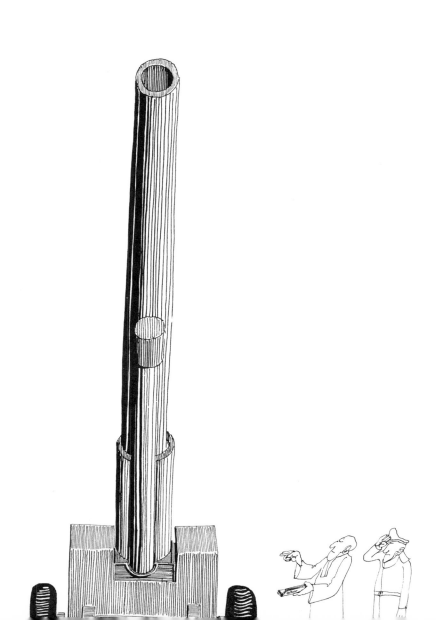

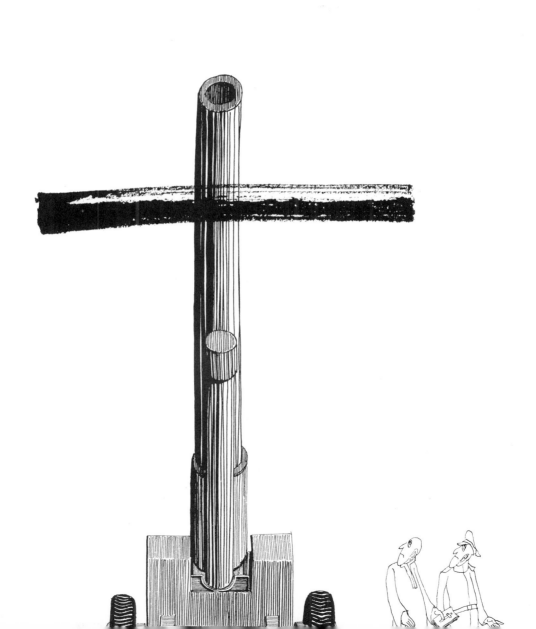